The Victory in Losing

©Kaz Antonio

The Victory in Losing   Kaz Antonio

This book is published by Casana Spence in 2015

Copyright © Casana Spence, 2015

Kaz Antonio has asserted his right under the Copyright Act, 1993 to be identified as the author of this work.

This book is sold subject to the condition that it shall not be recopied or reproduced in any form other than how it is sold.

First published in Jamaica in 2015 by Casana Spence, Falmouth, Trelawny

An official copy of this publication is available at the National Library of Jamaica
12 East Street
Kingston, Jamaica

ISBN 978-976-95797-2-9

This book is printed by Phoenix Printery
141 East Street
Kingston, Jamaica

Read other books written by Kaz Antonio

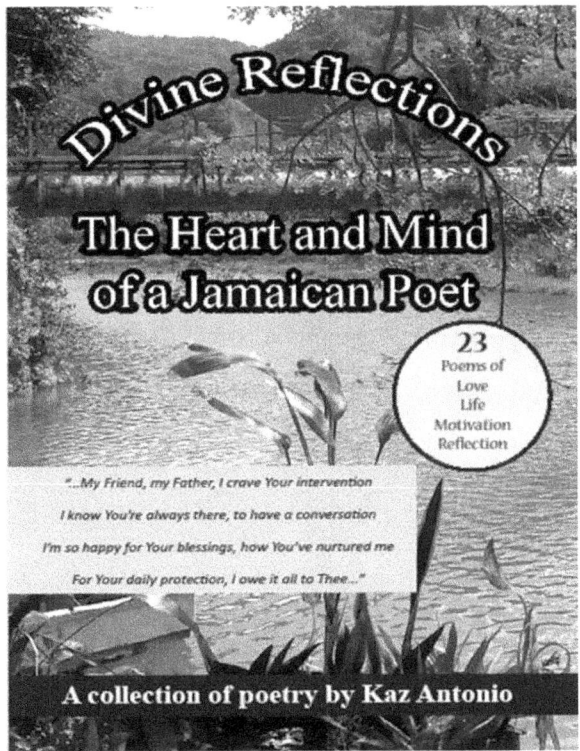

Find it on amazon.com or Bryan's bookstores in Jamaica

http://goo.gl/rop6CK

Content

Introduction	10
Foreword	12
Prelude	13
Running	14
Prelude	17
The School of Life	18
Prelude	21
The Child of a King	22
Prelude	24
Destination.....Montego Bay	25
Prelude	29
The Victory in Losing	30
Prelude	32
But You said you loved me	33
Prelude	35
Brother, Cry if you need to	36
Prelude	38
Conundrum	39

The Victory in Losing Kaz Antonio

Prelude	42
Hold that Thought	43
Prelude	45
I Feel your Pain	46
Prelude	49
Stand and be Counted	50
Prelude	52
Love Liberated	53
Prelude	55
Until you Arrive	56
Prelude	59
None of this Matters	60
Prelude	63
This Warzone of Life	64
Prelude	66
The Wind in my Sail	67
Prelude	69
When the Lion looks at me	70
Prelude	72
Stand up Woman!	73

Prelude	75
She Loves Him more than me	76
Prelude	78
No Peace without War	79
Prelude	88
I didn't have what Glittered	81
Prelude	84
Yes	85
Prelude	87
Get down off that horse	88
Prelude	90
Perfectly Imperfect	91
Prelude	93
She Died that day	94
Prelude	97
Want Me	98
Prelude	101
Before it's too late	102
Prelude	104
Noone else to blame	105

The Victory in Losing   Kaz Antonio

Prelude	109
The Year JPS stole Christmas	110
Prelude	112
What will your story be	113
End of Journey	116
Acknowledgements	118

Introduction

Losing isn't always losing, in fact there is great victory in ending up at the wrong end of our expectations. This book is entitled **"The Victory in Losing"** for this very reason. We are often disappointed because we miss the mark represented by being first, being the best or being recognized as the victor. There are so many life instances that teach us that in order to win sometimes we have to lose and to attain something great we first have to let some things go. Winning the war may involve losing some of the battles. Being a better person may mean losing yourself as you are. Seeing the bigger picture may mean losing sight of the smaller and less important things. God sometimes denies our requests or take us through a season of hardship in preparing us for a greater victory.

As I composed the various poems in this book each one was inspired by different experiences and meditations but the overall inspiration was undoubtedly Divine. Being allowed to encounter certain challenges or exposed to varying situations afforded me the opportunity to immerse my mind and heart in the moment and write. A group of simple and comprehensive words that communicate coherent thoughts is how I describe my poetry and this book. They are expressions, experiences and revelations that span across different levels and this is the objective of the literature. Different topics were written on, some of which take you into territories not covered in the previous book. However, there is a message for everyone and I dare you to expand your minds and see the positive message in each poem.

The pleasure is totally mine to be blessed enough to entertain your heart and mind with words placed on my heart to share. I hope I can accomplish this feat with at least one of the thirty poems in this book.

There is absolutely a greater victory in some of the losses we experience. It is also up to our willingness and ability to view even the most desolate experience in a positive way. Take a moment of reflection and ponder on all the times you 'lost'. How much did you gain or learn from those experiences? God Bless!

Foreword

It is often said "You have to lose to win". In this life, in order for us to enjoy true victories, we must embrace our setbacks. What is more important, we should use them not as stumbling blocks but as building blocks to get to the heights we need to be. The **Victory in Losing** speaks of just that – being victorious despite feeling like you have lost. It also speaks to how losing may just be your biggest win. This master-piece written by Jamaican Poet, Kaz Antonio will stir your soul and inspire you to never give out, give in or give up, no matter what struggles you are combatting. Irrespective of how daunting the challenge, you can be victorious.

"The LORD will fight for you and ye shall hold your PEACE"
Humans see loses but God guarantees victories. You will see yours despite "losing." **Shanelle Reid**

Prelude

The race is not for the swift but for those who can endure. It's not running to win but running to finish. Running from who you are and running to who you want to be. We have to run because we are constantly being chased. You're tired of standing and you're trying to get somewhere. We have to keep running because the end is near.

The Victory in Losing Kaz Antonio

Running...!

You're standing at the junction, you've been here so many times

You're sweating from this marathon you've been running all your life

Your energy is almost expended, your legs start to give way

Panting and grasping for breath for the words you want to say

But you keep on moving because the race is not for the swift

The drive continues, there's so much left to fix

You're running because you're tired of yourself

And you're strong enough to admit that you need some help

All the times you've tried to fix things on your own

Have done nothing but pushed you further from your goal

But there's too much at stake to give up now

The Victory in Losing Kaz Antonio

And you're running for dear life for Him to show you how

And each time you ask you're renewed in strength

The type of vigour that couldn't come from yourself

There's too much at stake to stop and quit

So you keep on running while you dry your sweat

And though the finish is far, you celebrate where you've come

Acknowledge your progress and smile as you run

You're running for today and the hope of tomorrow

Running from the past and to a future that's better

You can't stop running there's too much at stake

There's no time to reminisce or stop and complain

There are some tears in your sweat but lift up your hands

Because while you're still running you're defeating the devil's plans

Sometimes you will stumble and even get hurt

Body scarred with bruises and mouth filled with dirt

You have to keep moving don't stand in one place

Keep in your heart that you're covered by grace

Run like your life depends on it and this is literal

Run away from the life where sin is habitual

Run away from the lion and run towards Him

This is not a race to come first, it's a race that you must finish.

Kaz Antonio 2015

Prelude

Life teaches us lessons every day. Some we pass while failing some, until we eventually pass the ones we have failed. Life is like a school but there are no lesson plans and everything and everyone are our teachers. We all get the opportunity to attend this school but how we learn our lessons is dependent on us.

The School of Life

We get lost in the life we see, the life our eyes portray

Life can become monotonous, as we progress day by day

We often gaze in despair, and wonder if there is more

We fear diving into the ocean because it is safer on the shore

We say life is often cruel because we only live it one time

And if only we had the vision, that is as clear as hindsight

Life is just for living, this philosophy is held by some

Some say why worry about the future, take each day as they come

Life becomes a routine, when we live each day like the last

Then your heart is filled with regret, when forced to think on the past

Life is a series of events, it all depends on the approach

A combination of tests and blessings, how we build and grow

Whether happiness is your desire, or sorrow your reality

Examine your heart attitude, consider everything an opportunity

There is no point in living, if your mandate is regret

Strength lies in your ability, to quickly forgive and forget

Take time to meditate, look at life beyond your eyes

The Victory in Losing   Kaz Antonio

Listen to the voice within, and great things you'll realize

Don't be driven by fears, search for light in the darkness
Ask for Divine inspiration, to unleash your strength and greatness
You're not here to merely exist, be in pursuit of your purpose
Tackle your demons and goliaths, even in fear be courageous
When life rocks you back and forth, learn to ride the tides
Life isn't a smooth highway, there are odds for you to defy
As peaceful as the sea appears, the waves can be monstrous
So as easy as life can be, some seasons are often treacherous

As we lie down with the moon and rise up with the sun
Are we products of circumstances, do they shape who we become?
Do you see yourself as unfortunate, do each day you ask why me?
How do you embrace your life, is the glass half full or half empty?
Do you reshape like the clouds, how do you take the punches?
Are you stuck in the mud or victimized by circumstances?
Do you take grudges through life, castrate those who offend?
When all of this is said and done, what will be your life statement?

The Victory in Losing Kaz Antonio

Do you live in the fast lane, do you enjoy the journey?

Do you help others along the way, did you learn to say I'm sorry?

Are you as smooth as sea stones, or does life give you scars?

Do you live under the radar, or do you raise some bars?

Are you ever burned by the sun, or ever soaked in the rain?

Does life caress you dearly, does it protect you from all pain?

Were you prepared for all you encountered, did life open your eyes?

Do you learn some strong lessons, when you attend the school of life?

Kaz Antonio 2015

Prelude

Know who you are because you belong to royalty. All that is His is yours and you need to claim this in His mighty name. Don't let anyone speak defeat to you or convince you that you are less than you are. Know in your heart to Whom you belong and let this shine through your soul.

" In my Father's house there are many mansions. If it were not so I would have told you. I go to prepare a place for you." (John 14:2)

The Child of a King

No crown on my head but one in my heart

But I didn't know I belonged to royalty from the very start

All the times I've been tricked into believing something else

The many days that I struggled not knowing my true wealth

Thinking I'm impoverished when my Father possesses riches

So I rise up like the phoenix and ready to claim my blessings

I have not because I ask not so my petition is filled with faith

But I have to keep on working as I patiently anticipate

Sometimes I'm caught up worrying how or what will I eat

But the birds and plants are taken care of so why not me?

The Victory in Losing　　　　　　　　　　　　Kaz Antonio

I may not wear the royal garments but He looks beyond these things

I belong to the royal Kingdom of which He is King

So my walk has a little swagger because I can get anything I want

As long as my Father approves and in Jesus's name I chant

And I tell the devil NO, don't speak defeat to me

Because I'm the child of the King and I'll have the victory

No chariots parked outside nor do I have seven hundred wives

But I have more than enough to be thankful each day of life

Because this world is not my home, I'm being prepared for eternity

To live in and among mansions with the King and the family

Where gold paves the streets and angels are my friends

All my loved ones who passed on, I may very well see them again

So I can't care what you think of me because I know who I am

I more focused on where I am going than where I'm coming from

You may not see my crown but I will always sing

I am strong and mighty because I'm the child of a King

Kaz Antonio 2015

Prelude

Have you ever travelled on a public bus between Kingston and Montego Bay, Jamaica? If you haven't had this experience then pencil it on your bucket list, or not! This is an experience that develops so many aspects of your mind, body and soul. Oh boy! What an adventure this was en route to Montego Bay.

Destination...Montego Bay

I could have travelled in comfort, could have travelled in style

But my options became slim as I was very pressed for time

I travelled to Kingston for business and almost spent all day

Desperate to leave the city, I needed to get back to Mobay

I weighed the options keenly but left with only one decision

And I had to act swiftly to get to my destination

Travelled to the park in the crowd and sweltering heat

All the way thinking, I hope I get a good seat

For those who have had the experience they know what it means

To be crammed in a position where you can't feel your feet

So I stepped up on the bus trying to be optimistic

But this was quickly shot down when I saw things chaotic

I was fifth in a seat that could only fit four

By the time I got to Mobay everything would be sore

The Victory in Losing Kaz Antonio

So I conditioned my mind and took one for the team

Because in a few hours' time my home I would see

The bus was frustrating and everyone was shuffling

Adjusting for comfort everyone was cussing

So I thought happy thoughts and ignored the pain

But my discomforted companions could not do the same

The conductor ignored requests to redesign the flow

But the more they kept asking his head stayed outside the door

The lady complained that I was sitting on her hip

Another held her head down like she was about to be sick

But I kept thinking of the comfort I would have in a while

That all this would pass in a matter of time

When it wasn't the discomfort it was the driving pace

They cussed they would never reach home driving at this rate

Then the driver started driving at a speed so fast

Now the complaints shifted, the driver became the outcast

There was drama all around just like a soap opera

Who said what, who's with who, the little girl and her father

Open conversations in the Kingstonian accent

The hair, the nails, the tattoos and what is that scent?

The Victory in Losing — Kaz Antonio

So we finally got to St. Ann and they decided no more

That continuing in discomfort wouldn't happen for sure

The arguments ensued and threats exchanged

And from where I was I couldn't continue this way

Again I was weighing the options of what to do at this point

But I knew I couldn't endure the arguments and the fight

So I gave up my spot to restore some peace

And got off the bus now I don't know how I will reach

I remember singing the song "God will take care of me"

Even though I couldn't see the answer to where I wanted to be

So with my bag on my back I decided to walk

Because if I was to get an answer I needed to start

Got in a taxi that could hold no more

But the greedy driver decided to make three passengers four

Kept a smile on my face because all this must be for a reason

That there must be a story at the end of this season

I had to travel back in time and get another bus

This time I was comfortable and noone cussed

A destination that should've been three hours turned out to be six

A lesson well learnt that better doesn't mean quick

The Victory in Losing — Kaz Antonio

A time filled with drama, an action packed day

What a journey this was en route to Montego Bay

Kaz Antonio 2015

Prelude

Some of the most monumental victories derive as a result of losing. We make the association of winning with prizes, medals and celebration but sometimes to secure real and indelible victories losing is important.

How much or how big did you have to lose to win?

The Victory in Losing

Sometimes we battle with the sole mission to win the fight

We exert our best energies to prove what is right

We play the game not for the experience and fun

We only compete just to say we've won

But some of the greatest victories are experienced when we lose

Some of the best lessons are leant from the options we choose

Sometimes you have to lose the battle in order to win the war

And sometimes lose yourself to find out who you are

The loss of your riches may unveil the real treasure

Losing a life of fun may unlock true pleasure

Losing what you put first may cause you to gain God

Losing your secular crutches may strengthen your Christian walk

Losing what you have may get you what you need

Losing what you hold on to may realize your dream

Losing a loved one may create a protecting angel

Losing the world may gain you a home to dwell

The Victory in Losing Kaz Antonio

Losing an argument may earn you peace and tranquility

Losing your outer appearance may reveal your true beauty

Giving up your comfort may unearth your hidden gift

Losing your grip on reality may give you that spiritual lift

Losing your sleep may increase conversations with Him

Losing the fun and excitement may protect you from a life of sin

Losing your mind may cause you to gain your sight

You have to lose it all if you want to save your life

Kaz Antonio 2015

Prelude

There is no confusion about love even though it may be expressed in different ways. Love is kind, strong and sure and in the absence of these attributes one must question if love is that feeling that is possessed. Half-hearted, half expressed and withheld emotions are questionable, love is not.

If you love, then love!

The Victory in Losing

But you said you loved me...

You profess your commitment yet your love seems conditional

Told me you are mine but give your withdrawn affection

What true love can this be when I see through your empty stare

You are physically present but your mind is nowhere near

Your hugs are half-hearted, you seem confused of what you want

It's like you're trapped by I want to, but controlled by I can't

The words that are spoken, not a reflection of what you express

A love only given in part, never to experience your best

You refused to stand up when sitting down was wrong

You chose to be weak when it was time to be strong

You fixed your eyes on the past when the future was much brighter

You chose to accept defeat when you should have been a fighter

You focused on a dream and forgot about the mission

You doubted what was real, you questioned my ambition

The true love that you offered was gone with the wind

You allowed the devil to trick you in settling for the sin

I would have shared my life, perhaps you wanted the world

The Victory in Losing   Kaz Antonio

We could have found the treasures, much more precious than pearls

You said that you loved me and that there was no other

But that love crumbled when we could've been a force together

A love inflated with words, quickly eroded by just the smell of rain

A love that developed muscles cried from a hint of pain

But you said that you loved me, those words came from your mouth

Rest in peace sweet love, you were killed by sin and doubt

Kaz Antonio 2015

Prelude

Society says crying is a sign of weakness, especially for men. What a misconception this is! Crying expresses so many emotions and communicates so many sentiments. Is one to believe that we were given this ability to indicate that we are weak? If anything this defines the fullness of a man.

Brother cry if you need to!

Brother, Cry if you need to

They say tears is a sign of weakness and real men shouldn't cry

That crying is a feminine response and men shouldn't show that side

Masculinity is now in question, emotions have a gender

Like the boundaries are redefined, the divide seems so slender

When your child exceeds expectation, your heart bursts with pride

Hold them tight and express love, nothing's wrong if you want to cry

When God reveals His true love, such grace He continues to show

Lift your head and give Him praise, cry if that's what you know

When your daughter looks at you like you're superman in her world

So what if your eyes fill with tears, express that she's your girl

When your woman blows you away with deeds that fill your heart

The Victory in Losing Kaz Antonio

These things can melt you down and rips your ego apart

When you learn of world poverty and see the hunger in his eyes

If you're moved with deep emotions, tears may be your reply

A hundred killed in the storm and you see suffering and loss of lives

It's a perfectly human response for the pain to be seen in your eyes

Your mother finally hugs you and says I love you son

You find yourself humbled, where did all these tears come from?

The day you say I do when you know she's your better half

A truly joyful experience, you cry while you laugh

Brother cry if you want to, noone gets to judge

Cry if this is your response to pain, appreciation or love

Ignore the foolish notion that crying is for the weak

If anything it shows you're human, to be ashamed there's no need

Kaz Antonio 2015

Prelude

She played with fire and got burnt but the writing was on the wall. She was trapped by feelings that prevented her from letting go. It is important to develop the wisdom to identify harmful things from an early stage and make the decision to stay clear of what is created to harm us. Listen to the voice of reason within and save yourself the pain.

If you don't then....It's your fault

Conundrum

She met him the first day, they hadn't met before

By the way they connected she knew there'd be something more

She loved what he had, he brought a mist of comfort

It wasn't before long that she started calculating his worth

Day two was the same, they shared a hidden connection

A soft gentle smile, she felt like she belonged

Emotions got deeper, the connection grew intense

Her rationale told her NO but she tried to make other sense

She started to make assumptions, she listened to the little whispers

She had to keep reminding herself that this person wasn't hers

They smiled around the probable, noone would assume

They both played it safe while dispersing little clues

Sitting by the sea they discovered they both had a situation

By now everything else was clouded by what they had at hand

They continued at a different pace, the picture was more pronounced

The Victory in Losing Kaz Antonio

They ventured the inevitable, that Saturday she went to his house

Boldly they played with fire, noone would get burnt

Bearing all the factors, would anyone get hurt?

He did what became necessary to temper the other variable

And in the presence of the other, she became the controlled person

While she gave him the full circle, his was strategically designed

To adapt to the situation he knew how to manipulate minds

She grew in confusion, she wasn't in control of a lot

Her mind rambled back and forth, she was always on the spot

She was trusting and falling but her anxiety went north

But in hindsight she realized, this was all her fault

She kept on asking "is it me or is it her?"

He said she was as good as gone, something he failed to confirm

The situation grew too quickly, someone had to be used

Someone had to take the bait, one of them had to be fooled

Someone had to be in the dark, someone had to play

Someone had to be the shark, someone had to be played

Someone had to sit and wonder, someone had to know the truth

The Victory in Losing   Kaz Antonio

Someone had to wait and ponder, someone had to take the route

Someone had to feel the pain, someone had to fight

Someone had to lose the game, someone had to see the light

Someone had to make it to the end, someone had to halt

Someone had to stop the trend but she had to bear the fault

"I should've avoided the first day, I should've kept my head down

I should've had nothing to say, then noone would be the clown

I should've accepted things for what they were, avoid all the emotions

I never should've pursued more, just stopped at the introduction

I should've frowned and walked away, shouldn't have opened the vault

I should've arrived late the day, this was all my fault"

Kaz Antonio 2005

Prelude

"Whatever things are noble, lovely, praiseworthy fix your mind on these..." (Phillipians 4:8). While life has many things to keep us depressed all day it is also filled with enough blessings to make us strong and confident. Make an effort to replace negative thoughts with uplifting and positive ones and whenever you find something that fills your heart and mind with joy......

Hold that thought!

The Victory in Losing   Kaz Antonio

Hold that Thought!

"You'll never amount to anything, you're just like your father"

"There is no hope for you, you'll always be a cheater"

Thoughts from all angles saturating your mind

Such thoughts of negativity dominating your life

But you weren't given a spirit of shame, guilt or fear

You weren't given an attitude to live in despair

Learn to separate the things of God from those brought by the devil

The spirit of darkness will hold you back, making you feel incapable

Whatever thoughts are lovely and pure place your mind on these

And whatever struggles you face go down on your knees

Keep your mind on positive things, the devil will keep you depressed

He hates your strive for greatness, he prefers to keep you oppressed

Hold on to thoughts that make you strong, keep you moving today

Focus your mind on all those things that keep negativity away

If your mind is set on guilt and shame from something you have done

These thoughts are from the devil and not your Father above

If your mind is stuck on hurt that prevents your forgiveness

The Victory in Losing Kaz Antonio

That comes straight from the pit of hell we need to pass this test

Noone said the task is easy but be the commander of your mind

Hold its hand and lead it, just like you would a child

Hold the thought that uplifts, hold it tightly with security

Lead away those that suppress, they have no place in your mentality

Sing the thoughts of gratitude, there's always much to give thanks

Banish the thought that complains, let go of its hands

Repeat the thought that glorifies make it your daily chant

Remove the thought that upsets, this energy you don't want

Accept the thought that magnifies, you're nothing without Him

Deflect the thought that focuses on all acts of sin

Embrace the thoughts of truth, acceptance of your blessings

Release the thoughts of vengeance, focus on forgiving

Celebrate the thoughts of salvation, believe and humbly wait

Hold the thoughts of unfailing love, receive this gift through faith

Kaz Antonio 2015

Prelude

Terrorism and other acts of war have snuffed out lives from among us. These are mothers, sisters, brothers, fathers; these are families. We are all connected in some way regardless of geographic location and when the world is robbed of potential and promise it is indeed a tragedy.

I cry for my brothers and sisters because I feel their pain.

I Feel your Pain
A Tribute to lives lost from terrorism and acts of war

My brother and my sister, trust me I feel your pain

It didn't happen to me directly but I'm hurting just the same

Lives taken inhumanely, how do we begin to understand?

Crimes of the highest order, how do we rationalize this mission?

My brothers and my sisters when you cry I'm crying too

Because no one has the liberty to take lives from among you

There is no right or reason to disrupt your social order

No purpose can explain assuming this type of power

Hopes, dreams and potential gone in a matter of minutes

So much tears and anguish how can our hearts stand this?

I cry because you're hurting and we are all connected in some way

The Victory in Losing Kaz Antonio

My heart overflows with emotions, there are just no words to say

For all my people in Paris my heart goes out to you

Trust that our God isn't sleeping and He knows just what to do

For all my people in Kenya I offer you my condolence

Brothers killing brothers all this makes no sense

For all my people in Rwanda, it's been years but I remember

My hands go up to you for now standing strong together

For all my people in America, you have lost many innocent children

But you keep rising like the phoenix each time you have fallen

For all my people in Nigeria, I know they took your daughters

Such senselessness in the world, how do you console these mothers?

For all my people in Jamaica, we need to stop killing ourselves

Such a small and talented nation, none of this makes sense

For all my people in Cameroon, middle and Far East

I pray for unity and harmony so that all the war can cease

For all the nations in the world that have lost friends and family

Even if I can't relate exactly, I understand pain and tragedy

Over a hundred dead in Paris and many more injured

The Victory in Losing   Kaz Antonio

I lift my hands to Heaven and say a prayer for you

Over a hundred dead and so much hurting by extension

We all share a little pain because of our Divine connection

Over a hundred dead in Kenya, teachers and students alike

How can one be so simple about something as precious as life?

Brothers, sisters and friends, treated with such little regard

If we really ponder hard enough, what is the rationale for war?

The world has been deprived, a part of our family taken

People I feel your pain, from this my heart is broken

Kaz Antonio 2015

Prelude

If you want to progress you have to take responsibility for the pursuit of your success. If you're going to dream then might as well dream big but develop the attitude to chase what your heart believes. Fix your mind, get that look in your eyes and start working.

Stand up!

Stand and be Counted

Stand and be counted don't be a mere number in the room

Don't sit on your hands waiting for your dreams to come true

Stand up and stand out and let your voice be heard

Let your character be your identity and not just your words

Lift your head up and let your face be seen

Represent yourself so they can feel what you see

Look them in the eyes so they know who you are

Develop your self- worth so they can see you from afar

Strive to be the captain or the leader of the team

Exercise your perseverance so you become the chaser of dreams

Get that spark in your eyes for upliftment and progress

The Victory in Losing — Kaz Antonio

But learn very well that money doesn't measure success

Stand and be counted and lift up someone too
The world has more than enough to share the spotlight with you
And even if you're reserved and prefer to lead from behind
The world still has enough room to accommodate your kind
So even if you sweep the street do it to the best of your ability
Because pride and diligence beget a certain nobility
Don't be a fly on the wall let them hear you speak
Because all this time they swore that you were weak
You're not invisible or transparent you have fire blazing within
Let them know you belong to royalty, you're the child of a King
Some *'play possum'* when they're down and defeated
But that's the time to declare you broke but you're not broken
Stand and be counted and let your light so shine
So men will see your good works and know you as a child of Thine

Kaz Antonio 2015

Prelude

Love should not be caged or deprived of liberty. Let it grow like flowers in a garden. Nurture it so that it develops in the right conditions. Protect and treasure it so that it may be strong and produce fruits. Express it so it is always felt.

Liberate it!

Love Liberated

Whoever thought that love could be like this?

What started as a hug transformed into a kiss

It was innocent admiration, nothing more was aspired

That blossomed into attraction then so much was desired

Small and petite, I enjoyed your innocence

Focused and driven, I admired your confidence

So much mystery wrapped up in a woman

Understanding her persona became my mission

When our spirits collided it sparked a flame

That blazed so strongly with the passing of each day

Attraction turned to love filled with such excitement

And all that was simple converted to commitments

The Victory in Losing Kaz Antonio

When she curls up next to me and hugs me gently

It commands a protective embrace but done very softly

Love should not be caged and held in secret

It should be unleashed to the world even evident in public

I ask God to cover you and bless every aspect of your life

And to liberate all the love previously hidden inside

Kaz Antonio 2014

Prelude

I think about my unborn, not even conceived child and wait excitedly for the time when hopefully I will to be a father for the first time. I patiently and humbly wait and pray that God is preparing me to be the best steward for His child to which I will be the earthly father. I wait with faith and as obediently as I can.

I am being the best me for you!

Until you Arrive

I always dream of you and eagerly anticipate

In my darkest depression you put a smile on my face

I see your eyes and nose as you look back at me

A love that's unconditional lasting for eternity

I dream of holding you and taking you for walks

I envision my excitement for the first words you talk

But until you arrive I'll be making your home

An environment filled with love and so much more

I'll be creating a better person and being a stronger man

Working on my virtues so I can be the best dad

Securing all the things, waiting on my wife

The Victory in Losing

For us to build a stable home, needed for your life

Making God priority in all our pursuits

Keeping Him central so we'll bear good fruits

Correcting all I can before you arrive unto us

Removing circumstances that may be hazardous

Building an environment where you can grow up and play

Creating such surroundings where you'll be safe each day

Will I see myself in you, will you be like me?

Will I go overboard to provide everything you need?

Will you have my personality or be more like mom?

When you see me the first time will you know I'm dad?

I will give you all the love that my heart can extend

And I'll thank God daily for the blessing He sent

I will talk to you daily from inside mom's belly

Sing to you always, read you bedtime stories

Teach you about the world before your birth

Make you understand the depth of your worth

The Victory in Losing — Kaz Antonio

I'll be preparing your room whether blue or pink

Always thinking of you, imagining every wink

Until you arrive I'll keep you in my heart

My source of motivation, a light in the dark

You'll be born into a family with much love and care

I'll introduce you to our Father the moment you're here

And until you arrive you're being protected by Him

I'll meet you soon my love, I'll be here waiting

Kaz Antonio 2015

Prelude

In what do we place our value? We spend so much of our time worrying about material things when none of it has any true value. We often lose sight of what is important and these are the things and people in which we should entrust our value.

At the end of the day, does it really matter?

None of this Matters

I turn my eyes to the hills and I vanish from reality

Wondering about life, on the things we stress about daily

Narrowing my vision of life in its simplicity

Pondering on the things that contribute to our vanity

How much of this matters when it's all said and done

How much of this life do we really understand?

We worry about our figure or the style of our hair

About how we look to others or the fashion we wear

The car that we drive or the jewelry we own

The degrees that we have or the size of our home

The money that we have or the assets under our name

The Victory in Losing   Kaz Antonio

The company we have or the extent of our fame

The parties we keep or the places we've been

In the circle that we are or the tone of our skin

The jobs that we have or the money we make

The riches that we have or the house by the lake

Our status in life or the people we know

To the level that we rise and the people below

The size of the rock on the engagement ring

The diamonds on your wrist and the others places you bling

In the grand scheme of things none of this counts

With the wrong heart attitude to nothing this amounts

It doesn't matter who we are none of it can be taken

So while we hoard our treasures what values are forsaken?

None of this matters if we exalt ourselves

We possess nothing on this earth all of it is lent

While we enjoy always remember the source

And use it all for upliftment as we stay on the course

What we have doesn't matter, who we are is the test

So while we may have it all, always give your best

Kaz Antonio 2015

Prelude

Any given day could be our last because of the times we live in. It is indeed a warzone out there and the attacks come in different ways and different angles. Physical protection in not enough, we have to clothe ourselves spiritually.

"For we do not wrestle against flesh and blood but against principalities, against powers, against the rulers of the darkness of this age..." (Ephesians 6:12)

This Warzone of Life

Lord go before me and make my path straight

'Cause I'm fully aware that this could be my last day

This life that I live in awaits my destruction

So as I step out each day I pray for your protection

I'm living in a warzone, there is always an attack

So while my head is forward I ask God to watch my back

I'm walking around minefields, I'm cautious with each step

And if I succumb to the enemy this will cause my death

Even though we may not see them the enemy is always watching

The Victory in Losing Kaz Antonio

And sneak behind our defences without even giving a warning

Your demise is their mission so always stand guard

Don't be fooled by your own strength, always seek the Lord's

These weapons of mass *distraction* may make you lose focus

And tactics of intimidation may prevent you from being courageous

But stand firm in your conviction, keep moving even if you're afraid

And keep your eyes and ears open, the next attack is always near

This warfare is not carnal we are fighting powers and principalities

We are fighting legions of enemies that challenge our spirituality

They want us in chains and bondage, to make us their slaves

Starve us from bread and living water till we depart to the grave

To feed us with their doctrines that contradict the Holy One

To make us question His will, strip us of our freedom

This warfare is never ending but there's access to salvation

Strategies to become victors, tactics to fight temptation

So as you step unto the battlefield put on your helmet and sword

Our victory lies in the weapon, the weapon of the Holy Word

Kaz Antonio 2015

Prelude

My mother who fathered me! There is no greater blessing I have in life. The fan who is always cheering even when I am losing. I salute the person you have been throughout the years and the sacrifices you made for my dreams.

I couldn't have gone anywhere without the wind in my sail!

The Wind in my Sail
A Tribute to my mother

There was no success promised to me but I knew I had to pursue it

And if I were to make it far, giving up could not be a habit

I keep my vision firm while cognizant of reality

I keep the fire burning and always believe in my ability

While I drive towards my goals there are sources of motivation

One of which is great support, my mother's belief in her son

She scaffolded my dreams as a boy and even now as a man

Maybe I wouldn't be so determined without the support of my mom

Always standing in my corner even when my confidence was nil

Like a die-hearted fan always cheering me to win

She gave what she didn't have, so many miracles I remember

This woman is my everything, she's both mother and father

She didn't have what was required but she always found a way

The Victory in Losing   Kaz Antonio

Always provided the impetus for me to fight another day

She couldn't provide what glittered but she gave more than gold

A love that's never failing, needed fuel for my soul

My mother is my motivation and she lifts me as a king

Even when I have no words, she provides a rhythm for me to sing

Sometimes I didn't see how but she must have had a vision

One wish is that I've done her well, that she's proud of this man

So many lessons learnt, a lot of wisdom I've absorbed

Just by living in her attitude, I've learnt to remove *'I can't'*

My mother who fathered me, nourished my soul to make me strong

Her love that forms a circle, for her I thank God

Kaz Antonio 2015

Prelude

We all have to face our fears at some point especially when running isn't an option. Sometimes we defeat ourselves even before the fight begins so in essence, we can become our greatest enemy.

Stand up and fight today so you may not have to run another day!

The Victory in Losing Kaz Antonio

When the Lion looks at me

I'm anxious and scared as it prepares to attack

I brandish my brave face as I try to look back

That which I flee now has me in its grasp

Now I'm praying to be Daniel in the midst of this task

I'm lacking in courage and confess that I am weak

My entire body restless from the refuge I seek

It is either me or it but one of us has to die

And given my mission there's no choice but to survive

I may be weak in body but I have a seed of faith

And I have something inside that's mighty and great

So my eyes become wider and my stance becomes firm

Because if I don't fight this battle, I may never learn

How to be strong and never back down

To conjure up that strength that was previously unknown

My vision becomes clear as I size up the opponent

The Victory in Losing　　　　　　　　　　　　　　　　Kaz Antonio

And my heart becomes filled with bravado and encouragement

I step towards the lion, ready for the war

Fully prepared to give and take and walk away with some scars

The step becomes an advance, I'm not waiting for it to move

Between my heart and my mind I have something to prove

That I'm not fazed by its title or even its height

And it may be king of the jungle but I'm suited for this fight

My advance becomes a run, now going full throttle

Because if I'm ever to succeed I can't hide from this battle

Even if I lose this round I will always try

And when the lion looks at me, I stare right back in its eyes

Kaz Antonio 2015

Prelude

Women are the backbone of the nation and they should be respected dearly. They should be lifted up and celebrated for all that they are, and all that they help us be. They are strength and beauty defined. They are blessings gifted by God.

Stand up woman! Let us celebrate you.

Stand up Woman!

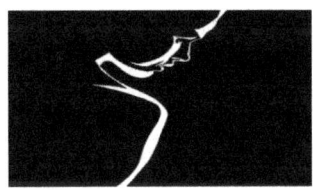

You carry so much than one can understand

But you maintain your femininity, so tender yet strong

You play so many roles and still keep it together

Friend, sister, counselor and still you're a mother

Sureness in your words, your attitude and eyes

Confidence in your walk, your finesse and poise

Experience in your conduct and your general approach

Strength in your perseverance and pursuit of your goals

Motivated by your vision held for your life

Fueled by your aspirations that push each stride

You instill pride and principles in your children

Teach them when they fall they must stand up again

You carry so much weight that's more than your frame

Superwoman and superstar but you seek no fame

The Victory in Losing Kaz Antonio

In so many ways you're there to our rescue

Without a strong woman what would a man do?

You give birth to our nation and develop its strength

You define its backbone and empower its existence

So I remove your hat and replace it with a crown

You're the daughter of a king and everyone should know

So stand up woman, for you and your family

Keep standing woman you inspire many

Thank you for your dreams, power and perseverance

A soldier you are while maintaining your appearance

Humbled by this gift God blessed to the earth

Stand up woman, incomparable is your worth

Kaz Antonio 2015

Prelude

How comfortable would a man be to have another man placed before him? She values everything more about the other man but she loves them both. Quite a predicament this is but nothing is wrong with accepting this situation.

Make sure she loves Him more than she loves you.

The Victory in Losing   Kaz Antonio

She loves Him more than me

She loves Him more than she does me, more attention He gets

In a normal situation one would be enraged and upset

She depends on Him for everything even though I'm her partner

Gives her commitment to Him even though I love her

She talks to Him every morning and many times per day

Even when I don't get a word, to Him there are always things to say

She talks to Him about me and our personal situations

As close as we are she shows Him greater obligation

Everyday she expresses love, she has open conversations

She doesn't care about my presence, she does it whenever she can

She asks Him for protection and for things I can't deliver

I know I'm not her first love, His power is far superior

Their relationship is close, even more than what we share

She always strives to please Him, to her heart He's very dear

She talks to Him all the time, even when I'm being ignored

I do my best to provide her needs but in His promises she's sure

The Victory in Losing Kaz Antonio

My love remains unwavering even though there's another man

I've learnt to accept many things, much more my heart understands

Although she gives me her best she gives Him so much more

At times she even cries for Him, she gives Him love galore

A love that's unconditional, if she had to choose it would be Him

A love I can't compete with, I wouldn't know where to begin

But I salute her commitment, putting nothing before this man

Regardless of what we share and where we're coming from

This love she has for Him makes me love her more

Because in all honesty, I too love Him more than I love her

Kaz Antonio 2015

Prelude

Many good things in life come after chastening. They are revealed after tests and trials and often results of fervent work and perseverance. No declaration of peace can be made unless there was existent war. Don't be afraid of opposition or adversity. After the darkness fades be ready to face the light. After the destruction caused by the storm watch the vegetation in your life reproduce with beauty.

Embrace war if you desire peace!

No Peace without War

Victory is celebrated after you triumph over a battle

Great lessons are often learnt after experiencing serious trouble

The abundance of life is seen after you could have lost it all

Your resolve is often stronger after you fall

The beautiful rainbow appears after the rain

Some of the happiness you enjoy is felt after pain

The pureness of gold is revealed after it's been through fire

Just like taking the bitter medicine before your health gets better

The strength of your character sometimes develops after hurt

Sometimes you have to be in the valley to know your true worth

You have to expend all your energy before you win the race

At times you have to be in the gutter before reaching a higher place

No peace can be declared if there was no war

There's no proof of being a soldier without a few scars

The strength of your relationship is tested by the wind

And if it's firm like the willow tree in adversity it will sing

You may never know inner peace till after the agony of confession

The Victory in Losing   Kaz Antonio

You may never find yourself till after the pain of isolation

True freedom is realized after first losing your liberty

Sometimes you have to lose yourself before finding your identity

Sometimes you have to stand behind before you become the leader

You have to battle the odds before being declared the winner

Sometimes to appreciate true wealth you have to know poverty

Sometimes you have to know real strangers to embrace family

Sometimes you have to be abandoned to develop your independence

Your awareness may be sharper after losing your keenest sense

Be a ball of burning heat that defines a star

In order to have peace sometimes there must be war

Kaz Antonio 2015

Prelude

Did you grow up with the silver spoon in your mouth or did you grow from humble beginnings? I know where I am going especially because I know where I am coming from. Be proud and be happy with what you have. Not because you had a certain start means that's how you will finish.

The world is filled with gold but what glitters for you?

The Victory in Losing   Kaz Antonio

I didn't have what Glittered

I didn't grow up with treasures, was brought up quite humbly

Didn't have the type of riches defined by society

I didn't have the house and car, didn't have the picket fence

Didn't go to the shopping mall or the fancy places people went

I didn't have the best shoes or expensive clothes people wore

Didn't have my own room or grew up with toys galore

I didn't have what glittered but I grew up with so much more

I grew around friends and family, to me that's as good as gold

So I didn't have the house on the hill or a life in the suburbs

But I had the type of childhood that was great and superb

I didn't grow up with fame and fortune but I had love in my home

So my foundation isn't built on sand but firmly grounded on stones

I didn't go to fancy restaurants, my food probably wasn't gourmet

But I never grew up hungry, there was always food on my plate

We didn't have the luxury car, an easy life I didn't know

But I grew up in an environment where my house was a great home

We didn't always have the answer of what to wear or eat

The Victory in Losing — Kaz Antonio

But my back was always covered, there was always shoes on my feet

My clothes didn't brandish brand names, my family didn't have a ton

But between the laughter and games, I grew up with loads of fun

We didn't have real estate or lots of saved up money

We had our poverty days but we always had family

I didn't fly to foreign countries, I didn't have those vacations

But I had God in my heart, Who prepared me for greater destinations

No grand birthday parties, no closet filled with presents

But I grew up with strong virtues, the teachings of a good conscience

No Genesis or Nintendo, no big screen TV on the wall

But I had marbles and box trucks not to mention gunwar*

The truth is I didn't grow up with much and this is honesty told

I didn't grow up with all that glittered, what I had was so much more

Kaz Antonio 2015

Prelude

The day came for the young man to stand up and step up to the plate. He was nervous but sure and this was his time. This was the time of his life and he had to deliver in a big way.

Have you had your moment where you had to step up?

Yes...

"Lord give me insight and guide my way for what I'm about to do"

This was his prayer as he got prepared, for a significant life move

Nervous in step but sure in heart, the mission was already decided

Nothing was normal, to how he knew, from the day their paths collided

But growth took place, in all areas, the vision became clearer

And as time progressed and desires deepen, the moment got nearer

Very meticulous, in making a choice, the request had to be strong

His search was assiduous, at times tiring, in finding the right one

So when it was time, to step up to the plate, to him it was already done

But as sure as he was of what to do, his heart pounded like a gong

Looking at the water so clear and blue, the plot and setting in place

Lights camera action, the time was here, it was time to take the stage

The Victory in Losing Kaz Antonio

He acted a while to throw her off, preparing his minds for the words

To change their lives, forevermore, imagine how his heart surged

He stared at the ocean to calm his nerves, so tranquil and inviting

He looked at her, she was all so clueless this moment was very exciting

The time was chaotic and not the best, the timing was not perfect

But the devil is a liar and up to him, he would've fled the moment

He composed himself, expressed to her, how they've grown over time

He shared his desires for both of them, the way he wanted her for life

He took one knee, opened the box, she placed her hand over her mouth

He took her finger, slid on the ring, to be her husband he had no doubt

She was in awe, paused a while, his heart was beating out of his chest

She looked at the diamond and nodded her head, yes.... she said yes

Kaz Antonio 2015

Prelude

Pride, ego and esteem. All these can cloud our judgement and attitude. In a world where we co-exist and depend on each other for one reason or the other our treatment of people can determine the type of relationships we share. Untouchable and invincible should never be used to describe anyone but unfortunately this is the attitude some exude.

Get off your high horse!

Get Down from that Horse

Too big or too strong sometimes we get too high

We carry too much ego, drunk on our own pride

Too important or too busy we can't lend a hand

Lost in our success, forgotten where we came from

Too rich or too esteemed we can't serve another

Can't even spend some time to help a fallen brother

Too known or too famous we become the worshipped

Swallowed by fake attention, we sever key relationships

Too rich or too established, we can't be seen with the 'little people'

Caught up in the fairy tale, living life like a fable

Too polished or too refined we can't get our hands dirty

We've lost the simple skills, we no longer have the ability

Too travelled or too revered, we can't embrace anything local

Self- inflated and selfish, we have become so egotistical

Too holy or too religious as if we are without sin

Taken the role to be God like any of us can be Him

The Victory in Losing Kaz Antonio

Too pretty or too attractive caught up with our self- worth

Completely lost the concept of what it means to be down to earth

Too fashionable or too stylish, we have to keep up the appearance

Built up ourselves as icons, we neglect the point of obedience

Too educated or too informed, we can't relate on certain levels

Created our wall and fences, locking everyone outside our circle

Too accomplished or too awarded, nose and chest aimed at the sky

Built up layers of self- protection, tricked that it's weak to even cry

Too hurt or too wounded, have gone through too much to forgive

Locked perpetrators in our hearts like this is any way to live

Too loved or too respected, we are on the mountain top

Forgotten the poor and deprived, make it harder to bridge the gap

Too blessed or too favoured this is often the talk

Let's abandon mere words, it's time to make that walk

Kaz Antonio 2005

Prelude

No two persons are exactly alike, physically or mentally. Embrace who you are and be proud. Work on yourself if this change will make you a better person for God and ask Him to help you accept the total you.

"I will bless the Lord for I am wonderfully and fearfully made. Marvelous are your works and that my soul knows very well." (Psalms 139:14)

Perfectly Imperfect

They may smirk at your smile or question your walk

Even ponder about your hair or the energy in your laugh

Confused about your dress or the style of your shoes

Disagree with your logic or the friends that you choose

Wonder about your eyes or the curl of your lips

Smile at your size or the bounce of your hips

But you're perfectly imperfect and you should be proud

Perfectly imperfect, you should say it out loud

You may hide the little flaws like the spots in your face

But you're beautiful regardless in so many ways

You may not have the perfect smile so you wear a frown

But you're the child of a King so you deserve a crown

You may be bigger than average so you're not courageous

But look at it positively you're curvy and voluptuous

You're not bold like the others, you get nervous when you speak

But use your other gifts to be the genius behind the scenes

The Victory in Losing   Kaz Antonio

You're perfectly imperfect let this be known

Perfectly imperfect make a joyful sound

You weren't made for speed so you don't run very fast

But when it comes to endurance you're ahead of this task

Your brain may be different you're not theoretically smart

But with all things practical this is completely your part

You're not physically inclined so you're not athletic

But you're great with your mind and very strategic

You make your mistakes just like everyone else

But your heart is pure and true and you're always yourself

Celebrate your gifts and talent and embrace your flaws

There is noone like you so stand very tall

You're perfectly imperfect, count this as joy

Perfectly imperfect, take these wings and fly

Kaz Antonio 2015

Prelude

She was tired of her life and decided to end it. She was exhausted of everything being the same regardless of how hard she tried. Life won't change until we decide to take a stand and admitting that our strength is not enough to fight the battles of the world.

> Give up! The fight is too big for us alone.

She Died that day

All the arrows had pointed that it must have been a curse

In all her efforts for transformation, sometimes she turned out worse

She headed down the same paths, those alleys seemed like home

Even in the midst of company, she would still feel alone

She grew tired of the live she lived for so many years

Laughter shown in public but in private it was tears

All the times she felt hurt she was in fact hurting herself

She became her greatest enemy, she didn't know how to ask for help

She would fill her flesh with pleasure, not knowing it was pain

She gambled with her life, thinking it was all a game

Buried herself in darkness she couldn't stand to face the light

Ignored what was important, she was lost in shame and pride

The Victory in Losing Kaz Antonio

How does she walk away from all that gave her comfort?

When all this vanishes away, what will define her worth?

She lost so many battles, she was tired of the fight

In her heart she had no option, she knew she had to die

Not that her life was bad but she knew she needed this release

A life in so much turmoil, she gave up and declared peace

She was ready to give it up and saw that life no more

She surrendered and removed her guard, a little doubtful but more sure

Recounted all she did, conceded to the fact

Decided to face the music when all her life she turned her back

She felt pain while it was happening but relief took control

She could feel herself dying but peace taking over her soul

Before she was comforted by the enemy because he felt like her friend

But there were so many times in hindsight, she was protected by angels

Her weapons weren't strong enough, so she always lost the war

Her world had been distracting so she often missed the Call

But to keep your life you have to lose it, she grew to understand

To live life her way was no longer her plan

The Victory in Losing Kaz Antonio

Lord deliver me from myself, she sat, cried and prayed

She became a different person, from the moment she died that day

Kaz Antonio 2015

Prelude

It's a great feeling to be wanted and appreciated by those we dedicate time and attention to. It is also important that you share the same vision for the direction of the union. Wanting each other represents all the things that both parties want in creating a coherent vision for the future.

Want Me

I submerge you in my mind, I take you in my dreams

I capture you inside, so you can feel the things I feel

I whisper things to you, feel it flowing down your spine

Your senses so aware, you muffle laughters like a child

Be silent, be still, listen to the verses I chant

I want your heart to be filled, I want you to want what I want

Hold my hand with desire, look at me with passion

Can you feel the heat of the fire, are you going my direction?

Sing the tunes of the rhythm, move your feet to the flow

Don't you hear our hearts ringing? Let's take it nice and slow

Close your eyes with me, let's fly away for a while

The Victory in Losing Kaz Antonio

Can you envision what I see? See the white dress down the aisle?

Let's dream but wide awake, lose not of reality

Do you believe in fate? People don't meet like this daily

I've seen a thousand pictures but only one consumes my mind

You're complete with all the features, a complex match to my profile

Let's combine our thoughts of tomorrow, embrace what's here today

Forget things of sorrow, let's bloom like daisies in May

Be true to the voice within, listen to the words of your heart

What do you really believe? Settle for what you really want

From the day we met, we felt a connection for each other

A gentle movement of our spirits, everyday became sweeter

The desires grew stronger, we developed such a bond

Our hearts became fonder, everything flowing like a song

As unique as her personality, as tender as her demeanour

Never felt emotions quite the same, I pledge everything to please her

I wish we keep seeing the same light, having the same thought

Suited for the same fight, battling the same war

The Victory in Losing Kaz Antonio

Crying the same tears, feeling the same pain

Escaping the same fears, sheltering the same rain

Walking the same walk, knowing my heart is true

Talking the same talk, wanting me like I want you

Kaz Antonio 2005

Prelude

Time waits on noone. The opportunity missed may never present itself again so capitalize on the present. It is easy to procrastinate and make plans for later but this is a practice that one should never be comfortable with. Life is short and precious and there is no time like the present. Some things once missed in the moment are gone forever.

Act before it's too late!

Before it's too late

Life can pass you by while basking in a moment

One word can represent many, when expressing certain sentiments

Delays can be necessary but sometimes tragic to wait

And you lose the opportunity because now it's too late

Time waits on noone it goes with the wind

So say what you need to before you end up regretting

Tell her you're sorry, no need to procrastinate

When you decide you're ready it might be too late

Tell him how much you care and how much you're proud

You may lose the opportunity when you decide to make it known

Express your appreciation, don't take it for granted

Here today gone tomorrow, you didn't say what you wanted

Release the hate from your heart, offer forgiveness

When it's too late you realize none of it made sense

Mend that broken relationship, strive to make it stronger

Make the effort to rebuild it before it's gone forever

The Victory in Losing   Kaz Antonio

Spend time with your children while you have them around

When they grow up and disperse the time can't be found

Break the habit that holds you back and threatens your life

Don't wait until you're broken before you open your eyes

Reach out to the ones you hurt and apologize for the pain

Seek redemption for your errors before it's too late

Spend time with your daughter show her a real man

Create that stability before she loses her direction

Express love each day like your last day is tomorrow

Instead of living in regret when you're hit with sorrow

Be in pursuit of your goals, learn to seize the day

Capitalize on your ambition before the dream is taken away

Kaz Antonio 2015

Prelude

He was committed and hopeful even when the signs were obvious. He remained true to the vow he had made to her and kept his love alive in spite of all that was happening with his marriage. Strength can be defined by the fight to stay or by making the difficult decision to walk away.

She said she loved him but she lied.

Noone else to Blame

She left him standing, he was weak and ashamed

But in this event he was the one to be blamed

He gave her so much and in return received so little

Even when she did him wrong, he was the one in trouble

He gave her jewelry on her birthday, perfume on Valentine

She gave excuses on their anniversary, absence at Christmas time

Her job was demanding so they really hadn't fought

But a little birdie revealed, she had more time than he thought

He loved her very much, she was his day and night

If loving her was wrong he didn't want to be right

Nothing was good enough or comparable to her worth

And he never stopped trying even though she treated him like dirt

The Victory in Losing Kaz Antonio

He bought her roses after work, each and every day

And she was always welcomed for the thanks she failed to say

She was really sweet sometimes but horrible on other occasions

Home was the ideal place for her to vent her frustration

She said she loved him very much but there was no depth

But being the person he was, he would simply just accept

Sometimes she made him breakfast even dinner too

She even took care of him the time he had the flu

She responded to his needs in the most unique way

That year she went all out on their anniversary in May

But all this was miles apart, he had stopped questioning her moods

It always evoked a temper, often times she would get rude

Most nights he slept alone for the better part of them

When he volunteered to get her she said she'll be taken by a friend

Was it a man or woman, he wasn't a jealous person

In an attempt to suppress his doubts, he believed he had no reason

At times he tried calling her but she was always out of range

He gave in to his doubts, he now believed something was strange

The Victory in Losing   Kaz Antonio

He asked if she was cheating, if she had someone else

She got upset for a week but it seemed like a defense

The truth sometimes hurts, he learnt that from a child

They both were in obvious pain, did she have something to hide?

She eventually addressed the issue and vowed her innocence

Then she topped it off with intimacy, that time was much different

If there was a puppet in the room, answer the million dollar question

His doubts were washed away but he was back at square one

She justified her tears, everything was much better

As a child when he was bad, he did everything to please his mother

But he became less doubtful amidst all the kindness and giving

He apologized for the accusation, he saw that he was mistaken

She started to come home earlier, said she had some time

Massage and pampered him, transformed into a good wife

Yes he was a still a puppet, small enough to fit in her palm

He refused to question her transition from rude to extremely calm

He found a letter in the bedroom it was written a week earlier

The Victory in Losing   Kaz Antonio

With kisses all over it and written on scented paper

He started reading the letter and realized it was for him

She didn't have spoken words but had much to say in writing

She wrote: ***I love you very much just give me some time***

To get over our problems then everything will be fine

Do not get upset because things are a little crazy

No matter what happens I'll always be your lady...

He became so relieved, he was stirred from within

But on the very last line he realized, the letter wasn't for him

She was standing at the door when he finished the letter

Her bag was half opened it seemed she forgot the paper

He asked if she still loved him while sitting on the bed

Tears came to her eyes then she slowly shook her head

He stood up smiling, she went for a bag

It was already packed and that was so long

She left him standing, he was weak and ashamed

But all the signs were clear, there was noone else to be blamed

Kaz Antonio 2005

Prelude

This is a comical poem about an observation made during a Christmas season. Christmas in Jamaica is a grand affair highlighted by bright and colourful lights, decorated homes, carols and general festive attitudes. During this time however, Christmas was missing.

This company stole Christmas!

The Victory in Losing   Kaz Antonio

The Year JPS stole Christmas

It was the night before Christmas as some Christmas stories begin

I've celebrated many seasons but this one had no feeling

September came, October passed, no Christmas feeling in November

Many agreed something was missing, there was no Christmas fever

Few Christmas carols and holiday cheers, it felt like regular times

As the season pressed on, Christmas was nowhere in sight

There were many discussions, many people felt the same

I wondered if on the twenty fifth, it wouldn't feel like Christmas day

Something was clearly wrong but I couldn't put my finger on it

And it wasn't just me, others didn't feel Christmas in their spirit

I remembered years before, this time was filled with excitement

There were carols all around and overflow of gifts and sentiments

I overheard conversations, many said the same thing

That something wasn't there, no vibe that Christmas would bring

I made the discovery as I drove around one night

The Victory in Losing

Kaz Antonio

And it all became clear, there were hardly any Christmas lights

No Christmas lights in this season? No wonder the feeling was dim

But people got scared when they pondered December's light bill

I remembered the feeling to see every house illuminated

This was indeed a tragedy because of the fear JPS created

People were saying in regular months how the bills were so high

So imagine what it would be when they ran those Christmas lights

So the season came and went as people opted for less

But the case was opened and closed, JPS stole Christmas

Kaz Antonio 2015

Prelude

We all leave a legacy whether or not we want to. What we do with our lives and how we live determine what our legacy will be and if what we leave behind matters to us then we need to be deliberate about our story.

Let's live our lives like it is gifted, not like it is owed.

What will your story be...?

When you reflect on your life as you rock in your chair

Or when someone takes you flowers as they cry at your grave

When it's all said and done and you gave life your best

What grade did you score on life's big tests?

Did you live for the experience and made it your story?

Or did you live for the fame and focused on the glory?

You will be pushed in a corner and forced to reflect

To search deep within to discover your true self

Will you be a story of success and beating the odds?

Or did you keep your hands in your pockets while kicking the sand?

Whenever your name is called how will people be moved?

Did you inspire another, did you light up a room?

The Victory in Losing — Kaz Antonio

Will you be known for your industry, always striving for goals?

Or will it be for your greed, always taking more?

Did you lift up a brother when he was falling down?

Were you the rock for a sister when noone was around?

What monuments did you erect, who was your master?

Did you make it on your own, did you glorify your Father?

Were you a sock on a hand, were you a slave?

Did you walk and talk the lessons of the importance of being brave?

Did you honour your responsibilities, did you stand up as a man?

Or will you be known as a coward, all the times you ran?

Did you ignite a nation or atleast those close to you?

Were you a model in the home, showing how and what to do?

Did you jump and touch the sky, did you reach for the stars?

Or were you scared of the height or feared you'd fall?

Did you kick down any doors or stuck it to *'the man?'*

Did you refuse to sit down when you felt you should stand?

Did you walk with pride and kept it all above table?

Did you stand up for what was right even though it meant trouble?

Did you take and make opportunities, were you a leader?

The Victory in Losing Kaz Antonio

Did you refuse to be quieted or seated in the corner?

Did you at times jump in the ocean even when you couldn't swim?

Did you give your best even when you couldn't win?

Were you selfless in your ways, putting others before self?

Did you make yourself available when someone needed help?

Were you bitter with anger, did you learn to forgive?

Did you release the guilt and pain so that you could live?

This isn't a story that is told or written as literature

It is the legacy left behind, what we imprint on each other

Will the sum of your life evoke a smile or frown

Let's not live out our days thinking, *"if only I'd known"*

Live for each other because life is more than we can see

And if we always give our best, that's what our stories will be

Kaz Antonio 2015

End of Journey

You took the journey and I'm happy you did. The joy that writing provides is indescribable at times and it is this type of release that keeps me going. Composing the ***Victory in Losing*** made me tap into diverse poems, some of which had been locked away for years. I made the decision to open up and write in areas that weren't exposed in the previous book, ***Divine Reflections: The Heart and Mind of a Jamaican Poet***. I've shared my perspective on love, motivation, spirituality and even infidelity because I believe the diverse reader can appreciate the versatility of writing. I thank God for these experiences.

Thanks for supporting this book and it is because of you why I keep pushing to produce my thoughts and feelings for public consumption. I hope you explore some your own emotions and express them in ways that you are comfortable or gifted. As you would have read, crying, celebrating, winning and losing are emotions and situations that we should feel open enough to share and express. Don't live according to the standards of society especially where those standards do not represent positive messages and upliftment. Face your lions, cry if you need to and the next time you experience loss, wait for the victory.

Read other books written by Kaz Antonio

Divine Reflections: The Heart and Mind of a Jamaican Poet

From Yaad to Abroad: A Young Jamaican's story of Survival, Manhood and Success.

Broke but not Broken

Find them on Amazon.com or email kazantonio1@gmail.com for your copy.

Acknowledgements

I thank God for the gift of writing and expression through this form. He is the source of my motivation and inspiration and I give Him all the honour and glory. Thanks to:

Shanelle Reid for reviewing, editing and writing the foreword

Krishain Thompson and Andre Sterling (Kris n Drae) for their artistic work in promoting this book.

For all the persons, friends and family who supported the previous book- ***Divine Reflections: The Heart and Mind of a Jamaican Poet***, you helped to disperse the message across the world and your support is invaluable. Thanks to Sheldon Smith, Danika Barti, Hyacinth Brown-Shaw, Claudine (Sharon) Patterson, Georgia Luckoo and so many others for pushing my work forward. Thanks to Nicola Fagan for investing in my dream at a time when it was nothing but that. My sisters in Christ, Victoria Hamilton and Audrey McIntosh for helping to push my literature and reminding me not to limit God.

Thanks to my mother who was the first one to read my book. You remain the "Wind in my Sail" (poem#73). That one should explain the depth of my love and appreciation. Thanks to everyone for supporting the dream of Kaz Antonio/Casana Spence. It's never about the messenger, but the message!

About the Author

Casana Spence, whose pseudonym is ***Kaz Antonio*** resides in Jamaica, West Indies. His passion for writing and his love for the natural environment have seen him compose books of poetry as well as books for more expansive reading. His training in the areas of Education, Training, Marketing and Hospitality have played a part in the development of his literature. He is actively engaged in the professional roles as Marketer, Educator and Trainer but writing is the activity that truly makes his character come alive.

His dependence on his spiritual relationship with Christ keeps him grounded and he acknowledges God for everything he accomplishes. Follow his journey through the various channels provided in this and all his books.

www.ingramcontent.com/pod-product-compliance
Lightning Source LLC
Chambersburg PA
CBHW060841050426
42453CB00008B/772